Fake Love

GEORGE HATCHER

CasaHatcherPress

Introduction: A Note from an Imperfect Man

Let me be clear right from the start: I am not an expert on love. I'm not a therapist or a guru, and I have no interest in pointing fingers or telling anyone how to live their life. I can only speak from my own experience, and what a wild experience it's been.

The fact that my wife, Molly, and I have been married since 1965 is nothing short of a miracle. I say that because for the first half of our life together, I was a mess. I made mistakes—big ones. My ambition often outpaced my resources, leading to a series of business failures and white-collar crimes that landed me in jail not once, but several times. I was a wild person, and through it all—the bad checks, the court dates, the 42 months I eventually served for false bank entries—Molly waited for me. She was there. Always.

This book is about the difference between a love that endures and one that shatters at the first sign of trouble. I know that difference intimately. Before Molly, I was married three times; one of those marriages lasted just 24 days. I know what it's like when things fall apart. But my life with Molly has taught me what it means to hold things together. The love I have for her, and she for me, is the reason we survived the storms that would have, and should have, wrecked us. It's the anchor that allowed for the "miracle turn-around" in the second, much cleaner and happier, half of our life.

So when I talk about "fake love" in these pages, I'm not judging anyone. Many people in such relationships might already know it. I'm simply exploring the contrast. What I call "fake love" is fragile. It's the relationship that ends at the first argument, the first financial struggle, the first real test. Real love, as I've been blessed to experience it, is something else entirely. It's the force that withstands failure, humiliation, and even prison bars. It's the bedrock that remains when everything else has been washed away.

This book is my attempt to explore that difference. It's a collection of observations from an imperfect man who, by some grace, found a love so real it saw him through the worst of himself and into the best of his life.

Dedication

For Molly,

In a life of fleeting fireworks, you have always been the pilot light. The steady, quiet flame that kept me warm and guided me home. Thank you for being the gold in all my broken places.

All my love, always, George

This book can be purchased at over 40,000 bookstores and libraries including brick and mortar stores, online, in print and digital, including Apple, and Kindle. Casa Hatcher Press is a subsidiary of Pretty Face, Inc. Rancho Mirage, California 92270.

Casa Hatcher Press. http://casahatcherpress.com (800) 416-6189

Book and cover designed by Casa Hatcher Press

Fake Love by George Hatcher

First Edition August 2025

ISBN: 979-8-9996764-8-1 PaperBack

ISBN: 979-8-9996764-7-4 eBook

Also By George Hatcher

Mario 1: Woman in Jeopardy

Mario 2: Coming of Age

Mario 3: Risky Business

Mario 4: Free Fall

Mario 5: Afire

Mario 6: Marked

Mario 7: Aftershock

Mario 8: Captivated

Single Titles

One Wilshire

Gabi

Rico

Cats: Meow Is The Language Of Love

HER: Artistic Expressions Through AI

Elegance In White: Through Wedding Gowns

Quinceañera Fashion: Fifteen & Fabulous

Billion Dollar Rainmaker Part I

Pages of Passion Book 1: My First 19 Years

Pages of Passion Book 2: Bold Beginnings

Pages of Passion Book 3: Rising Waves

Pages of Passion Book 4: Threads of Destiny

Beyond The Scale: Health Benefits of Keto for Wellness

Cool Under Pressure: Warm With Humor

Love Is What It Is: Lessons From Everyday Life

Living Fully While We Wait to Die: Mindfulness Amid Mortality

Ignite Your Potential: Break Free From the Ordinary

AfterLight: A Voice Beyond The Grave

Coming Soon

Chapter 1: The Great Love Hoax

With the story you've just read in the introduction, you can understand why my 60-year partnership with Molly feels like it was forged in fire. The love we share isn't a fairy tale; it's the sturdy, time-tested reality that serves as my anchor.

That's why, when I look at the landscape of modern dating, I feel like I'm looking at a different planet. It seems to be a world of what I can only call 'fake love'—a grand and glittering hoax. It's a fast-paced game of fleeting distractions and superficial connections, and frankly, it looks exhausting. From the vantage point of a love that has survived everything, the whole endeavor seems designed to leave people feeling more alone than ever.

The Heart's Deceptions in a World of Swipes

. . .

The game often starts with what I'm told is the "Tinder trap." It promises endless potential connections right at your fingertips, but what it often delivers is a series of interactions that lack any real depth. It's the illusion that the next best thing is just a swipe away, so why invest in the person right in front of you? People find themselves on a carousel of awkward dates and mismatched expectations, all while chasing the high of a new match.

The problem is, this system encourages us to confuse a biological spark with a genuine connection. It's easy to mistake lust for love when you're judging a person based on a handful of perfectly curated photos and a clever one-liner. Lust is the flash of lightning; it's exciting and immediate. Love is the slow, steady rain that follows, the kind that actually nourishes the ground so something real can grow. In this modern game, it seems many are so busy chasing the lightning that they never stick around long enough for the rain.

Love in the Age of Disappearing Acts

This brings me to another phenomenon that baffles me: ghosting. In my day, if you weren't interested, you had the decency (or at least the courage) to say so. Now, people simply vanish without a trace, like a magician's disappearing act. One minute you're sharing memes and flirty texts, and the next you're left wondering if the whole thing was a figment of your imagination.

This isn't just about bad manners; it's a symptom of a culture that treats people as disposable. These disappearing acts are the natural consequence of surface-level relationships. When a connection has no roots, there's nothing to hold it in place. It fosters an environment of fake affection where authenticity is the first casualty. How can you build trust with someone if you're half-expecting them to become a ghost? Real love is about showing up, staying present, and choosing to work through things—not just vanishing when it gets inconvenient.

A Chapter 1 Reflection: Unmasking Your Own Search

Before we go further, it's worth taking a moment to think about this. The first step in avoiding a trap is knowing you're in one. Ask yourself:

1 What am I *really* looking for? Is it a temporary distraction and a bit of fun, or am I genuinely seeking a deep and meaningful connection? There is no wrong answer, but being honest with yourself is the most important first step.

2 When have I felt most authentic in a relationship (of any kind)? What were the circumstances? What did it feel like to show your true self, imperfections and all?

3 In my own actions, how do I distinguish between love and lust? How do I treat people when I'm simply infatuated versus when I truly care for their well-being?

. . .

Thinking about these questions won't magically solve the problem, but it will give you a compass. In a world selling a fantasy, the most powerful thing you can do is get clear on your own reality. In the next chapter, we'll look closer at the "hotness factor" and how prioritizing looks can be the first, and most deceptive, step in this great love hoax.

Chapter 2: Lust at First Sight

Believe me, I understand lust. In my younger days, before I learned the difference between a thrill and a foundation, I chased my share of shiny objects. I know firsthand how a pretty face or a spark of chemistry can feel like the most important thing in the world. It's a powerful, intoxicating force. But I also know, from the wreckage of three failed marriages, that it's a terrible architect. You can't build a life on a flash of lightning; you need something that will stand up to the storm.

Lust at first sight is where the great love hoax often begins. It's the easiest trap to fall into because it's biological. It's exciting. It's a roller coaster that's all thrilling drops and no slow, steady climb. But the ride always ends, and if that's all there is to the connection, you're left standing on the platform, a little dizzy and alone.

The Hotness Factor and the Chemistry Conundrum

. . .

In today's world, it seems this initial spark is everything. The "hotness factor" reigns supreme. People meticulously curate their appearances online, and we're conditioned to swipe right on the most polished profiles. It's the allure of being seen with someone deemed 'hot'. But what does that really get you? In my experience, a relationship built only on looks is like ordering a beautifully plated dish at a fancy restaurant only to discover that it tastes like cardboard. The excitement fades, and you're left craving something with actual substance.

What I find beautiful in Molly after 60 years has very little to do with the snapshot of the woman I married in 1965. The beauty I see now is in the lines around her eyes that map our shared laughter and tears. It's in the comfort of her presence that got me through my darkest days. That kind of beauty doesn't fade; it deepens. It's a beauty you'll never find if you're only chasing the "hotness factor."

The same goes for that elusive thing people call "chemistry." It can feel like a magical, sugary rush that sweeps you off your feet. But a sugar rush inevitably leads to a crash. Many of my early mistakes in relationships were built on that rush—confusing a fleeting, biological reaction with a true emotional bond. When the passion is all-consuming, it can blind you to the fact that you have nothing in common, no shared values, and no ability to communicate when things get tough. A real, lasting connection isn't a sugar rush; it's a slow-cooked meal. It takes time, patience, and the right ingredients to develop a rich and satisfying flavor.

Love's Awkward Little Brother: "Friends with Benefits"

. . .

This modern idea of "friends with benefits" strikes me as another offshoot of this confusion—a fiasco born from prioritizing lust while pretending it's something more convenient. It's an attempt to get the physical intimacy of a relationship without any of the vulnerability, commitment, or emotional heavy lifting.

But intimacy is more than an act; it's a state of being. It's about knowing and being known. When you try to isolate the physical part, you often end up with a connection that leaves you feeling more empty than satisfied. It's like trying to have a fireplace that gives off heat with no fire. It misses the entire point. In a true partnership, physical affection is an expression of a much deeper bond —a bond of trust, respect, and shared history. It's not the foundation; it's one of the beautiful rooms in a house that you've built together.

A Chapter 2 Reflection: Looking Beyond the Spark

If you want to build something that lasts, you have to be able to see beyond that initial, blinding spark of lust. Take a moment to ask yourself:

1 What qualities, beyond physical appearance, do I find genuinely and lastingly attractive in a person? Think about character, humor, kindness, or intelligence.

2 Think of a time you felt strong "chemistry" with someone. What was it really made of? Was it just physical attraction, or was it a shared sense of humor, intellectual excitement, or emotional understanding?

3 What does emotional intimacy mean to you? How does it differ from physical intimacy, and what role do you want both to play in your life?

Learning to distinguish the flash of lust from the steady glow of love is a crucial skill. It's the difference between chasing a firefly and navigating by the North Star. One is a fleeting distraction; the other can guide you home.

Chapter 3: Surface Tension

In my day, you got to know a person face-to-face. You learned about them through their stories, their handshake, the way their eyes lit up when they talked about something they loved. There were no online profiles to manage, no photo filters to apply. The only "highlight reel" was the memories you built together, good and bad.

Today, it seems we live in an age of immense surface tension. Everyone is curating a perfect public image, especially when it comes to relationships. This creates a pressure to live up to an impossible ideal, a myth of perfection that can make real, messy, beautiful love feel inadequate. It's a world built on glittering surfaces, and the tension comes from the fear that one wrong move, one crack in the facade, will cause the whole thing to shatter.

Instagram vs. Reality: The Perfect Relationship Myth

. . .

If Molly and I had social media in the early years of our marriage, our life wouldn't have looked like the perfect couples you see on Instagram. You wouldn't have seen pictures of us on exotic vacations with flawless tans and witty captions. You would have seen the harsh reality of struggle: Molly waiting for me outside a county jail, us trying to rebuild after one of my business ventures imploded. That was our reality. It wasn't pretty, and it certainly wasn't perfect.

This is the danger of the "perfect relationship myth." We scroll through feeds filled with curated moments—the sunset kiss, the anniversary dinner, the laughing selfie—and we mistake that for the whole story. It's a facade. Real life happens between those snapshots. It's in the arguments and the compromises. It's in the quiet, un-photogenic moments of support when one person is falling apart and the other is there to hold them up. Love isn't a highlight reel. It's the raw, unedited footage of a life shared, and chasing an illusion will only leave you feeling hollow when the cameras are off.

The Shiny Object Syndrome

I know a thing or two about chasing the "next big thing." In my business life, it nearly destroyed me. I was always pursuing the next shiny object, the can't-miss deal that I was sure would be the one, and that chase led me down a road of bad decisions and, eventually, to a prison cell. I learned the hard way that the things that glitter the most are rarely gold.

I see the same destructive impulse in modern dating. People are constantly looking over their partner's shoulder for someone newer, more exciting, or "better." It's the "shiny object syndrome" applied to human hearts. But a relationship isn't a trend you can trade in for a new model. A real partnership is something you build, brick by painful, loving brick, over time. It's an investment. By constantly chasing the next thrill, you never give anything real a chance to grow. The greatest treasure of my life wasn't a business deal; it was the woman who stayed, the one who proved that her value was in her steadfastness, not her novelty.

A Chapter 3 Reflection: Breaking the Surface

Escaping the pull of the superficial requires an honest look at what you're chasing and what you're afraid of. Ask yourself:

1 How does the life I present online compare to the one I actually live? In what ways am I curating an image for others?

2 What "shiny objects" (people, lifestyles, possessions) tend to distract me? What am I hoping to find in them that might be missing in my life right now?

3 What am I most afraid of showing to a potential partner? What are the "imperfect" parts of my story that I try to hide? Could those be the very things that allow a real connection to form?

True connection doesn't happen on the surface. It happens when we have the courage to break that tension, to let people see the messy, complicated, and authentic reality underneath. It's a risk, but it's the only way to find a love that's real enough to last.

Chapter 4: The Showdown: Learning the Difference

〰️

If there is one lesson that has taken me a lifetime to learn, it's this: you must understand the difference between love and lust. Confusing the two is like mistaking a firework for a star. One is a spectacular, noisy explosion that lights up the night for a brilliant moment and then vanishes into smoke. The other is a quiet, distant, steady light that can help you navigate your way home in the dark. In my youth, I chased fireworks. It took me years of getting lost to finally appreciate the stars.

This is the ultimate showdown, not between two people, but within yourself—the battle between the heart and the hormones. It's a clash that determines whether you build something that lasts or something that blows up on the launchpad.

When Lust Wears a Love Mask

. . .

Lust is a master of disguise. It feels exhilarating, all-consuming, and desperately important. It can look and sound so much like love that you'd swear it was the real thing. I should know. My first three marriages were built on the shaky ground of lust. They were whirlwinds of passion and excitement. They were also hollow.

The consequence of this confusion is that you build a life on a foundation of sand. When the tide of real-life problems comes in—and it always does—the whole structure washes away. With those early relationships, the connection was all about the good times, the thrill, the physical attraction. The moment real challenges appeared, there was nothing holding us together. The "love" we thought we had was just a mask, and underneath, we were two strangers who didn't know how to weather a storm. That disillusionment is a profound kind of heartbreak.

Spotting the Red Flags

Looking back, the red flags in those lust-driven connections were obvious, even if I chose to ignore them at the time. A relationship built on lust, not love, often shows these signs:

• **It's all about the present thrill.** The focus is on the physical connection and the immediate excitement. Conversations about the future are vague, fantastical, or avoided entirely.

• **Conflict is a dealbreaker.** Hard conversations are swept under the rug because the connection is too fragile to handle them. Real problems, financial stress, or personal struggles are seen as buzzkills, not challenges to be faced together.

• **The connection is conditional.** The affection and attention are there when things are easy and fun, but they vanish at the first sign of trouble. The ultimate red flag of a lust-based connection is a partner who disappears when the chips are down.

And then there was Molly. Our connection wasn't just a firework; it was the pilot light. When my life truly exploded—when the businesses failed and the jail doors closed—all the fireworks were long gone. But that small, steady flame of her love and commitment? It never went out. It was the one thing that kept the house from going cold and dark. That's how you know the difference. Lust runs from trouble. Love runs *toward* it.

A Chapter 4 Reflection: Examining Your Own Connections

This is the most critical distinction to make in your own life. Be honest with yourself as you consider these questions:

1 Describe a time you confused love with lust. What were the "red flags" you can now see in hindsight? What were the ultimate consequences of that confusion?

2 In your current or past relationships, what has been the "pilot light"? What are the quiet, steady, and reliable signs of connection that keep things warm, even when there are no fireworks?

3 How do you and your partner (or how have you in the past) handle conflict and crisis? Do you face it together, or does it push you apart? What does that tell you about the foundation of your relationship?

Answering these questions can be tough. It requires a level of self-awareness that many of us, myself included, have had to learn the hard way. But it's the only way to stop chasing sparks and start building a real fire.

Chapter 5: Fairy Tales and Follies

If my life were a fairy tale, the book would have been slammed shut and thrown in the fire about halfway through. The idea that love is a magical journey to a perfect "happily ever after" is, from where I'm standing, one of the most dangerous fantasies we're fed. It's a myth that sets us up for failure and disappointment, making us discard real, imperfect, and beautiful connections because they don't fit a childish script.

My life with Molly is the furthest thing from a fairy tale, and that is precisely what makes our love so strong. It wasn't bestowed by a fairy godmother; it was forged in the fires of crisis and built with the hard bricks of forgiveness and commitment.

The Myth of "Happily Ever After"

. . .

"Happily ever after" sounds like an ending, a prize you get after you find the right person. That's a folly. A real partnership doesn't have an ending until one of you is gone. It's a continuous process of choosing each other, day after day, especially on the days when it's hard.

Our "happily" wasn't found in a castle; it was found in the decision to keep going after my business collapsed. It was reaffirmed in the visiting room of a county jail then later a prison. It was rebuilt from the ashes of my failures. Happiness, in a real and lasting love, isn't a destination. It's the shelter you build together to get through the storms. Believing in a magical, effortless "ever after" is a trap that stops people from doing the hard work that real happiness requires.

Prince Charming or Just a Pumpkin?

Let me be brutally honest about my role in our story: I was no Prince Charming. For a long stretch of our life together, I was the pumpkin, waiting to be turned into something better. I was the guy who made the messes, who broke the promises, who ended up on the wrong side of the law. A woman looking for the flawless hero of a fairy tale would have—and should have—run from me at top speed.

This is the poison of the Prince Charming myth. It makes people search for perfection, for a person with no flaws, no baggage, and no history of failure. That person doesn't exist. Real love isn't about finding a perfect partner. It's about seeing the potential for a king in an imperfect man and having the strength and grace to stand by him while he figures out how to wear the crown. It's about finding someone who sees your flaws and loves you not in spite of them, but because of the person you are becoming as you overcome them.

The Damsel in Distress Has Left the Building

If I wasn't Prince Charming, then Molly was certainly no damsel in distress. The woman in those stories is helpless, passive, and waiting for a man to rescue her. That wasn't Molly. In our story, she was the one with the sword.

She wasn't waiting for a rescue; she *was* the rescue. Her strength didn't lie in her weakness, but in her incredible resilience. She was the one fighting to keep our family, our future, and our hope intact while I was busy trying to destroy it all. She rescued our life not from a dragon, but from the consequences of my own actions. The narrative of the helpless woman is an insult to the strength of real partners. A true partnership is about two people standing side-by-side, taking turns saving each other when needed.

A Chapter 5 Reflection: Rewriting Your Own Story

Breaking free from these myths requires you to become the author of your own, more realistic story. Ask yourself:

1 What "fairy tale script" are you subconsciously following

or waiting for in your own life? (e.g., waiting for a grand gesture, a "rescue," or an effortless "happily ever after.")

2 Are you searching for a "perfect" partner? What flaws in others do you see as dealbreakers that might actually just be signs of being human? What flaws in yourself are you trying to hide?

3 In what ways are you waiting to be "rescued" in your life or relationships? And in what ways can you be your own hero, or recognize the strength of a partner who is anything but a damsel in distress?

The best love stories aren't fairy tales. They are real-life epics of grit, forgiveness, and two imperfect people who refuse to give up on each other.

Chapter 6: Authenticity in the Age of Filters

After you've had your failures and mistakes laid bare for the world to see, you learn a thing or two about authenticity. You learn that it's not a mask you put on to seem "real." It's what's left when all the other masks have been burned away in the fires of your own making. In an age of digital filters that smooth out every flaw, I've come to believe that true authenticity is found in the scars, not the seamless facade.

The modern world makes it easy to hide. We can filter our faces, curate our lives, and present a version of ourselves that is shinier and less complicated than the truth. But a real connection cannot be built between two avatars. It requires two real, imperfect people to have the courage to show up as they are.

The Real Deal: How to Spot Genuine Love

. . .

In a world of performances, how do you spot the real deal? You stop listening so much to what people say, and you start watching what they do. Talk is cheap. Promises are easy to make when the sun is shining. The real test of love is consistency, especially when it's inconvenient.

I learned to spot genuine love by watching Molly. Her love wasn't in grand declarations; it was in her unwavering presence during my deepest failures. It was in her choice to stay when everyone else would have left. That's the real deal. It's not a feeling; it's a verb, an action, a commitment that shows up day after day. A partner who is only there for you when it's fun and easy is like a gym membership you only use when the weather is nice. The real measure of a partner is if they'll spot you when the weight gets heavy.

Vulnerability: The Not-So-Secret Ingredient

People talk about vulnerability as if it's a secret ingredient you can choose to sprinkle into a relationship to make it better. For me, it was never a choice. It was the main course. When you're standing in front of a judge, or when you have to tell your wife you've lost everything again, there's no room for a brave face. You are stripped bare of all pretense.

That kind of forced vulnerability is terrifying. You are showing someone the absolute worst, most broken parts of yourself. You expect them to run. But a miraculous thing can happen. When they don't run—when they look at your exposed, flawed, authentic self and stay—that's when a bond of trust is forged that is stronger than steel. It's in that moment, when you have nothing left to hide, that you create a space for a love that is truly fearless. It's radical honesty, born of necessity, and it's the only soil in which a deep connection can grow.

Beyond the Lingo: A Love That Acts

I hear people talk about "love languages" and relationship jargon, and I suppose there's some truth in it. But you have to be careful that it doesn't become another filter, another way to perform love instead of living it. It's easy to get caught up in analyzing whether someone is showing love through "acts of service" or "quality time."

What was Molly's love language? It wasn't a term from a book. Her love language was "I'm not leaving." It was an action, a simple and profound statement made not with words, but with her life. Genuine love transcends lingo. It's in the quiet support, the shared knowing glance, the hand you hold when you're scared. Let's not get so lost in the jargon that we forget to recognize the simple, powerful truth of a love that shows up.

A Chapter 6 Reflection: Finding Your Authentic Self

Authenticity starts with being honest with yourself before you can be honest with anyone else.

1 What are the "filters" you apply to your own life? What parts of yourself are you most afraid to show a partner?

. . .

2 Think of a time you were truly vulnerable with someone. What happened? What did you learn from the experience, whether it was good or bad?

3 Beyond words, how do you *show* love and support to the people you care about? How do their actions, in turn, show their love for you?

In a world that pressures us to be perfect, the most radical act of love is to embrace our own, and our partner's, messy, beautiful, unfiltered humanity.

Chapter 7: The Road to Real

〰

The road from a life of fleeting connections to building something real is not a superhighway; it's a dirt track you have to clear yourself, one rock and one tree root at a time. It's a journey I know well, from the short-lived chaos of my early marriages to the 60-year partnership I've built with Molly. Understanding the difference between love and lust is the map, and authenticity is your compass. But to actually get anywhere, you have to be willing to do the work.

This is where the real journey begins. It's about making the conscious decision to stop chasing temporary thrills and start building a home for your heart.

From Flings to Things: Choosing to Build

A fling is easy. It's a rented motel room—exciting for a night, but you wouldn't want to live there. Building a real "thing"—a lasting, meaningful partnership—is like laying the foundation for a house. It's slow, unglamorous work. It requires patience, a shared vision, and the effort to dig deep, even when the ground is hard.

For Molly and me, the choice to build came after the storms had washed everything else away. We couldn't rely on the thrill of a new romance; we had to rely on a shared commitment to building a future out of the rubble of my past. This is a choice everyone has to make. You have to intentionally shift your focus from immediate gratification to long-term investment. It means filtering out connections that are only about the surface and looking for a partner who is willing to pick up a shovel and help you build, no matter what the weather looks like.

Communication Over Charades

You cannot build a house with someone by playing charades. You have to talk. You need blueprints, plans, and the ability to solve problems together. The same is true for a relationship. I see people today relying on gestures, memes, and vague cues, all while avoiding the conversations that matter.

Let me tell you, you can't play charades when you're discussing how to survive after a prison sentence. You have to use your words. You have to be brutally honest about your fears, your failures, and your hopes. Molly and I had to have conversations that were terrifyingly real. That kind of communication forges intimacy that a thousand flirty texts could never replicate.

. . .

Real communication isn't about tiptoeing around the truth to avoid a fight. It's about trusting your partner enough to tackle the truth together. It's the glue that holds everything else together. Without it, you're not partners; you're just two people guessing what the other one is thinking.

Finding Your Tribe, Even If It's a Tribe of One

People talk about the importance of "finding your tribe." In my darkest hours, my tribe had a population of one: Molly. She was my community. She was the one who showed up. This taught me that the strength of your support system isn't in its size, but in its loyalty.

Finding your tribe, whether it's one person or a dozen, isn't about finding people with the same hobbies. It's about finding people who share your core values—values like commitment, resilience, and unconditional support. These are the people who see you at your worst and don't flinch. They are the ones who form the bedrock of a truly rich and authentic life. In a world full of fake connections, a single, genuine alliance is worth more than a thousand superficial friends. Look for the people who aren't just there for the party, but who will help you clean up after the house burns down.

A Chapter 7 Reflection: Starting the Work

Building something real starts with small, intentional actions:
   1 What is one concrete step you can take *today* to invest

in a real connection, whether it's with a partner, a friend, or a family member?

2 What difficult but necessary conversation have you been avoiding? What is your fear, and what would be the first step in broaching the subject?

3 Who is in your "tribe"? Who has proven, through their actions, that they are there for you unconditionally? Take a moment to acknowledge what that support means to you.

The road to real is built not with grand gestures, but with the courage of a thousand small, honest, and consistent steps.

Chapter 8: Embracing Imperfection

Our world is obsessed with perfection—the perfect body, the perfect career, the perfect relationship displayed in a perfect Instagram post. It's a fool's errand that leaves everyone feeling inadequate. I should know. My life has been a masterclass in imperfection. And through it all, I've learned that the most beautiful things in this world are not those that are flawless, but those that have survived being broken.

Embracing imperfection is perhaps the most difficult and most important part of the journey to real love. It's where the fantasy of perfection dies and the beauty of reality begins.

The Beauty in the Breaks

For years, I tried to hide my flaws. I projected an image of a successful entrepreneur, a man who had it all under control, even as my life was spiraling. That attempt to maintain a perfect facade is what led to my biggest mistakes and my deepest pain. It was only when my imperfections were laid bare for the world to see—when my failures were undeniable—that I could finally start to build an honest life.

There's a Japanese art form called Kintsugi, where broken pottery is repaired with lacquer mixed with powdered gold. The idea is that by embracing the flaws and breaks, you make the object more beautiful and valuable than it was before. The cracks become a celebrated part of its history. My marriage to Molly is a work of Kintsugi. The breaks—my failures, my time in jail—are part of our story. They are not things to be hidden. Our love is the gold that holds the pieces together, and it is more beautiful for having been broken and repaired.

Loving the Whole Person

It's one thing to learn to accept your own flaws. It's a much greater challenge to truly accept your partner's. It's easy to love the parts of a person that are shiny and admirable. It takes real love to embrace the parts that are difficult, messy, and broken.

I gave Molly every reason to see me as nothing more than the sum of my mistakes. She could have defined me by my worst moments, and no one would have blamed her. But she never did. She saw the whole person. She knew my potential and my goodness even when I was buried under a mountain of my own bad choices.

. . .

This is the ultimate act of love: to see someone's imperfections clearly and choose to love them anyway. It's to understand that their scars are part of their story, just as yours are part of yours. It's a love that doesn't demand perfection because it knows that our flaws are what make us human, and overcoming them together is what makes a partnership divine.

A Chapter 8 Reflection: Finding the Gold in the Cracks

Learning to embrace imperfection is a practice, not a destination. It starts with compassion for yourself and for others.

1 What imperfections in yourself are you struggling to accept? How could you begin to see them not as sources of shame, but as part of the Kintsugi of your own life story?

2 Think of a person you love. What is one of their "flaws" that you can choose to embrace with more compassion? How does that imperfection contribute to who they are as a whole person?

3 How can you create a "safe harbor" in your relationships where both you and your partner feel comfortable being imperfect? What would that look and feel like?

When you stop chasing the illusion of perfection, you open yourself up to the profound, resilient, and honest beauty of a love that is real.

Chapter 9: Conclusion: The only Takeaway That Matters

We started this journey talking about my 60-year marriage, and it's only fitting that we end there. I've spent this book exploring the landscape of what I call "fake love"—the superficial connections, the confusing sparks of lust, the impossible fairy-tale standards. But looking back at these pages, I realize I wasn't really writing about fake love at all. I was writing a thank you note to a real one.

Everything I've learned about the difference between a fragile connection and a lasting one, I learned from my life with Molly. It's a lesson that was forged in failure and sealed by forgiveness. If there is one single takeaway from my story, from this entire book, it is this: Real love is not something you find in a state of perfection. It's something you build in a state of imperfection.

It's not a firework; it's the pilot light that keeps the house warm through the winter of your failures.

. . .

It's not a fairy tale; it's the gritty, real-life epic you write together, full of monsters you have to face as a team.

It's not a flawless diamond; it's the beautiful, golden repair of Kintsugi, where the cracks become the most valuable part of the story.

The journey to that kind of love requires you to stop chasing shiny objects and start doing the work. It demands that you trade your fear of vulnerability for the strength of authenticity. And most of all, it asks you to believe that you, and the partner you choose, are worthy of love not in spite of your flaws, but because of the grace and courage you show in embracing them.

So, what is the future of relationships? I have no idea. But I know that the fundamental truth of human connection does not change. In any era, in any landscape, the principles are the same.

Choose honesty over performance.

Choose commitment over convenience.

Choose a partner who chooses you, especially when you are at your worst.

In the end, my advice is simple. Forget about finding the perfect person who will make your life a fairy tale. Instead, find someone who will help you clean up after the house burns down. Then, spend the rest of your life building a new one together, brick by honest brick.

About the Author

George Hatcher's life is a testament to second chances. With a formal education that ended in the ninth grade, he has navigated a life of extreme highs and devastating lows, learning his most profound lessons not in a classroom, but through trial and error.

The first half of his life was a whirlwind of entrepreneurial ventures —some successful, others leading to catastrophic failures and, ultimately, prison. Through it all, the one constant, the anchor in every storm, has been his wife, Molly. Their 60-year marriage is the bedrock upon which the second half of his life—one of stability, peace, and prolific writing—was built.

As a passionate storyteller with over two dozen books to his name, George writes from a place of hard-won experience. He explores themes of love, loss, failure, and forgiveness, not as a theorist, but as a man who has lived them. He believes his greatest mistakes have been his most profound teachers and shares his story with unflinching honesty.

He currently resides in Rancho Mirage, California, with Molly, their three cats, and a macaw named Peaches. Now devoted entirely to his craft, George invites readers to join him on a remarkable journey that proves beauty isn't found in perfection, but in the strength it takes to repair what is broken.

A longer bio is available on his website: http://georgehatcher.com/bio/bio.html

www.ingramcontent.com/pod-product-compliance
Lightning Source LLC
Chambersburg PA
CBHW071352130626
46556CB00005B/2150